Too Cute!
Baby Wolves

by Elizabeth Neuenfeldt

BELLWETHER MEDIA
MINNEAPOLIS, MN

Blastoff! Beginners

Blastoff! Beginners are developed by literacy experts and educators to meet the needs of early readers. These engaging informational texts support young children as they begin reading about their world. Through simple language and high frequency words paired with crisp, colorful photos, Blastoff! Beginners launch young readers into the universe of independent reading.

Sight Words in This Book

a	in	many	they
and	is	new	this
are	it	play	to
at	like	see	will
big	look	the	
have	make	them	

This edition first published in 2023 by Bellwether Media, Inc.

No part of this publication may be reproduced in whole or in part without written permission of the publisher. For information regarding permission, write to Bellwether Media, Inc., Attention: Permissions Department, 6012 Blue Circle Drive, Minnetonka, MN 55343.

Library of Congress Cataloging-in-Publication Data

Names: Neuenfeldt, Elizabeth, author.
Title: Baby wolves / by Elizabeth Neuenfeldt.
Description: Minneapolis, MN : Bellwether Media, 2023. | Series: Blastoff! beginners: Too cute! | Includes bibliographical references and index. | Audience: Ages 4-7 | Audience: Grades K-1
Identifiers: LCCN 2022012991 (print) | LCCN 2022012992 (ebook) | ISBN 9781644876749 (library binding) | ISBN 9781648347207 (ebook)
Subjects: LCSH: Wolves--Infancy--Juvenile literature. Classification: LCC QL737.C22 N48 2023 (print) | LCC QL737.C22 (ebook) | DDC 599.773--dc23/eng/20220321
LC record available at https://lccn.loc.gov/2022012991
LC ebook record available at https://lccn.loc.gov/2022012992

Text copyright © 2023 by Bellwether Media, Inc. BLASTOFF! BEGINNERS and associated logos are trademarks and/or registered trademarks of Bellwether Media, Inc.

Editor: Christina Leaf   Designer: Jeffrey Kollock

Printed in the United States of America, North Mankato, MN.

Table of Contents

A Baby Wolf!	4
Pack Life	6
All Grown Up!	20
Baby Wolf Facts	22
Glossary	23
To Learn More	24
Index	24

A Baby Wolf!

Look at the baby wolf.
Hello, pup!

Pack Life

Pups have many brothers and sisters. They live in **packs**.

pack

Pups sleep in **dens**. Dens are in the ground.

den

Pups cannot see right away.
They nap a lot!

napping

Pups drink mom's milk. Later, mom brings them food.

Pups like to play. See them **wrestle**!

wrestling

Pups learn to **howl**.
They are loud!

howling

Pups learn to hunt. They follow grown-up wolves.

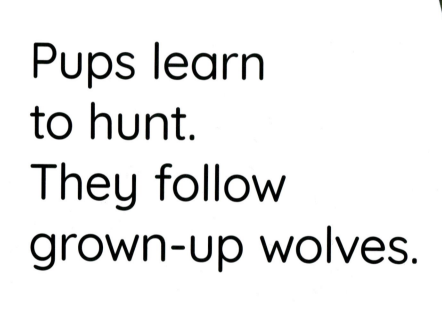

All Grown Up!

This wolf is big.
It will make
a new pack.
Goodbye, mom!

Baby Wolf Facts

Wolf Life Stages

pup   young adult   adult

A Day in the Life

nap   drink mom's milk   play

22

Glossary

dens

homes for wolves

howl

to make a long, loud sound

packs

groups of wolves

wrestle

to fight by grabbing and holding

To Learn More

ON THE WEB

FACTSURFER

Factsurfer.com gives you a safe, fun way to find more information.

1. Go to www.factsurfer.com.

2. Enter "baby wolves" into the search box and click 🔍.

3. Select your book cover to see a list of related content.

Index

big, 20
brothers, 6
dens, 8
drink, 12
follow, 18
food, 12
ground, 8
howl, 16, 17
hunt, 18

learn, 16, 18
loud, 16
milk, 12
mom, 12, 13, 20
nap, 10, 11
packs, 6, 7, 20
play, 14
see, 10, 14
sisters, 6

sleep, 8
wolf, 4, 18, 20
wrestle, 14, 15

The images in this book are reproduced through the courtesy of: Shutterstock, front cover; Eric Isselee, pp. 3, 4, 5, 22 (pup); blickwinkel/ Alamy, pp. 6-7; Geoffrey Kuchera, pp. 8, 23 (den); Janet Horton/ Alamy, pp. 8-9, 22 (nap, play); Jim Brandenburg/ SuperStock, pp. 10-11; Linda Smit Wildlife Impressions/ Alamy, pp. 12-13, 22 (drink); Danita Delimont Creative/ Alamy, pp. 14-15; Jason Hahn/ Alamy, p. 16; Michael Deyoung/ SuperStock, pp. 16-17; Design Pics/ Alamy, pp. 18-19; KenCanning, pp. 20-21; Arto Hakola/ Alamy, p. 22 (young adult); photomaster, p. 22 (adult); critterbiz, p. 23 (howl); Danita Delimont/ Alamy, p. 23; Bildagentur Zoonar GmbH, p. 23 (wrestle).